W9-BOL-733

Author:
Ian Graham studied applied physics at City University in London. He then received a postgraduate degree in journalism, specializing in science and technology. Since becoming a freelance author and journalist, he has written more than one hundred children's nonfiction books.

Artist:
David Antram was born in Brighton, England, in 1958. He studied at Eastbourne College of Art and then worked in advertising for 15 years before becoming a full-time artist. He has illustrated many children's nonfiction books.

Series creator:
David Salariya was born in Dundee, Scotland. He has illustrated a wide range of books and has created and designed many new series for publishers in the UK and overseas. David established The Salariya Book Company in 1989. He lives in Brighton with his wife, illustrator Shirley Willis, and their son, Jonathan.

Editor: **Stephen Haynes**

Editorial Assistant: **Mark Williams**

PAPER FROM
SUSTAINABLE
FORESTS

Published in Great Britain in 2012 by
The Salariya Book Company Ltd
25 Marlborough Place, Brighton BN1 1UB

ISBN-13: 978-0-531-20871-7 (lib. bdg.)   978-0-531-20946-2 (pbk.)
ISBN-10: 0-531-20871-0 (lib. bdg.)   0-531-20946-6 (pbk.)

All rights reserved.
Published in 2012 in the United States
by Franklin Watts
An imprint of Scholastic Inc.
Published simultaneously in Canada.

A CIP catalog record for this book is available
from the Library of Congress.

Printed and bound in China.
Printed on paper from sustainable sources.
1 2 3 4 5 6 7 8 9 10 R 21 20 19 18 17 16 15 14 13 12

SCHOLASTIC, FRANKLIN WATTS, and associated logos are
trademarks and/or registered trademarks of Scholastic Inc.

You Wouldn't Want to Work on the Hoover Dam!

Written by
Ian Graham

Illustrated by
David Antram

Created and designed by
David Salariya

An Explosive Job You'd Rather Not Do

Franklin Watts®
An Imprint of Scholastic Inc.
NEW YORK • TORONTO • LONDON • AUCKLAND • SYDNEY
MEXICO CITY • NEW DELHI • HONG KONG
DANBURY, CONNECTICUT

Contents

Introduction

You are a construction worker in Amarillo, Texas, in the 1920s. You have been working on construction sites since you left school nearly 10 years ago. You enjoy working outside, even when the weather isn't great.

Amarillo is doing well. Gas and oil were recently discovered nearby, so energy companies are setting up businesses and there is plenty of construction work to keep you busy. You are able to do most of the jobs that have to be done on a construction site, from general laboring to simple carpentry and laying concrete.

YOU DON'T KNOW it yet, but your world is about to come crashing down. It will happen suddenly and without warning. Soon, the United States will be overwhelmed by a disaster that will affect banks, businesses, and workers all over the country. It will change your life forever. You will find yourself in a different state, working on one of the biggest construction projects in American history.

The Crash

New York City is 1,550 miles (2,500 km) from Amarillo. You have never been to New York, but events happening there will turn your life upside down. The New York Stock Exchange on Wall Street is a bustling hall where traders buy and sell shares in companies. Investors make fortunes as share prices rise and rise during the 1920s. Then, in October 1929, share prices suddenly drop. Wealthy people see their fortunes disappear overnight. Companies all over the country go bust, and millions of people lose their jobs. Many go on protest marches to demand work.

You're fired!

THE EFFECTS of the stock market crash spread very quickly. When the boss arrives at your construction site, you fear the worst.

Give us our money!

BANKS START to fail, and people rush to take their money out. This makes a bad situation even worse.

PEOPLE who can't afford gas for their cars hitch them to horses instead. These horse-drawn cars are nicknamed Hoover wagons after U.S. president Herbert Hoover—many blame him for the economic disaster.

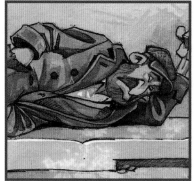

MANY PEOPLE lose their homes because they cannot pay their bills. They have to sleep on the streets.

JOBLESS MEN KEEP GOING
WE CAN'T TAKE CARE OF OUR OWN

TOWNS that don't have enough jobs for their own citizens put up signs telling the jobless people from other places to stay away.

MANY ARE SO POOR that they can't even buy food. Thousands stand in breadlines to be given free soup and bread.

CHILDREN march to demand jobs for their fathers. (At this time it's not common for women to work outside the home.)

Handy Hint

Hitch a free ride on a freight car to look for work in other towns.

WHY CAN'T YOU GIVE MY DAD A JOB?

UNGR

RICH KIDS DON'T STARVE WHY SHOULD WE?

Good News

While you are traveling from town to town looking for work, you hear about an exciting new construction project. The world's biggest dam is going to be built across the Colorado River. Arthur Powell Davis of the U.S. Reclamation Service thought of it. He suggested building the dam to supply surrounding states with water and to stop the Colorado River from flooding. It's such a huge project that six of the biggest construction companies in the United States join forces to build it. You set off for Nevada in the hope of finding work on the dam.

Either Too Much or Too Little!

FLOODS: Every spring, snow melting high up in the Rocky Mountains drains into the Colorado River. The swollen river overflows its banks and floods farmland farther downstream.

DROUGHT: Meanwhile, land farther away is as dry as a desert. Farms here badly need a reliable water supply.

PRESIDENT HERBERT HOOVER has been the driving force behind the project since he was U.S. secretary of commerce. It has taken years to get approval for the dam from Congress and from all the states affected by the plan.

Handy Hint

Take plenty of water with you when you're traveling across the desert.

This has possibilities!

Arthur Powell Davis

Ragtown

You hitch free rides on trucks and trains to get to Nevada. At a small desert town called Las Vegas, men like you are arriving from all over the country. Many have brought their families with them. Some of them stay in Las Vegas, but many others live in tents near the Colorado River. The ramshackle tent city becomes known as Ragtown. You visit the place where the dam will be built and find a deep canyon with a river at the bottom. It's hard to believe that a giant wall of concrete will be built across it.

There's nothing here at all!

SURVEYORS map every inch of the canyon. They make drawings that show the precise shape of the canyon walls where the dam will be built.

PEOPLE BUILD HOMES in Ragtown from whatever materials they can get their hands on. Many of them pitch tents, but others build shacks out of wood, rocks, metal sheeting, canvas, and even cardboard!

STOREKEEPERS set up businesses in Ragtown to serve the people's needs. The bakery is one of the busiest stores, because everyone needs bread.

THERE IS NO WATER SUPPLY in Ragtown. To get water, people dig holes in the riverbank. The holes fill with muddy water, which is collected in a bucket or saucepan.

WHEN YOU NEED to go to the bathroom, you have to use an open ditch called a latrine. The stench is nauseating.

LATRINE

11

An Army of Workers

Every morning you join crowds of men at the employment office, hoping to be hired to work on the dam. Up to 5,000 men at a time are employed on the dam. During the five-year construction project, a total of 21,000 workers are hired. They come from nearly every state, and there are some from overseas, too. The largest numbers are from California and Nevada—about 5,000 from each state. There are more than 600 Texans like you. There are truck drivers, carpenters, miners, electricians, mechanics, blacksmiths, welders, crane operators, power shovel operators, and many others.

MANY of the jobs done by your fellow workers are known by nicknames (some are more polite than others):

Truck drivers are "double-uglies."

Electricians are "juicers."

Bosses are "easy-doughs."

Laborers who scrape mud off the ground are "muckers."

Carpenters are "wood-butchers."

Workers high up on the canyon walls are "high-scalers."

EMPLOYMENT OFFICE

IT'S YOUR LUCKY DAY! You've been hired as a general laborer.

Chug
chug

Handy Hint

Don't let your tools out of your sight, or someone may steal them.

WORKERS TRAVEL to and from the construction site in buses. One bus is a mammoth 150-seat double-decker called Big Bertha.

A BLACK MUTT born on the site becomes the dam's mascot. He goes from worker to worker for a pat on the head. He eats his meals with the workers and he can even climb ladders!

I've been hired!

A NEW POLICE FORCE, the Hoover Dam Police Department, is set up to keep order in the new town of workers.

13

Diverting the River

Before the dam can be built, the Colorado River has to be diverted out of the way. This is done by sending the river through four tunnels in the canyon walls. The tunnels are carved out by explosives. Holes are drilled in the rock, then packed with explosives. The explosions shatter the rock. Every 14 feet (4 meters) of tunnel takes a ton of dynamite. The finished tunnels are as big as four-lane highways. Finally, the river is blocked by dumping rock and soil in the canyon. This forces the water into the tunnels.

THE DRILLING is done by workers on huge platforms called drilling jumbos.

Yikes!

MANY WORKERS DIE after being hit by rocks and other objects falling from the canyon walls.

BUILDING MATERIALS are brought up the river by boat until roads and railroad tracks can be built.

BOOM!

Handy Hint

Tie a wet rag over your mouth and nose to protect yourself from dust, smoke, and truck fumes.

A MEMORIAL commemorates 96 workers who died in accidents while building the dam. Another 20 or so died from other causes, including heatstroke, heart attacks, and pneumonia.

WORKING CONDITIONS in the canyon are terrible. The temperature can reach a blistering 140°F (60°C) in summer, and fall below freezing in winter.

15

Pay Day

Pay Rates

WORKERS ARE PAID according to which job they do. The pay rates range from 50 cents to $1.25 per hour.

Laborers
50 cents

Boat operators
62½ cents

Miners
70 cents

Mechanics
75 cents

Power shovel
operators
$1.25

The 10th and 25th of each month are your favorite days, because that's when everyone is paid. The workers go to the paymaster's office and stand in line at a window to be given their wages. Laborers like you earn 50 cents an hour and work for eight hours a day. That comes to $4 a day. You can make $1,460 in a year. It might not sound like much, but it's six times more than a farmworker earns. At a time when so many people all over the country are out of work, you consider yourself very lucky to have a job.

Four dollars a day! I'm rich!

WHEN WORKERS ARE HURT, they go to one of two first aid stations. If their injuries are serious, they are taken to a 20-bed hospital built specifically for the dam project workers.

Handy Hint

You have to work hard for your money, so don't gamble it away on card games.

Glug

THIRSTY WORK. Young lads called water boys run around the site giving bags full of water to the workers to quench their thirst.

High-Scalers

After starting off as a general laborer, you work as a mucker for a few weeks. Muckers clear mud and rock out of the bottom of the tunnels that are being dug to divert the river. It's a filthy, smelly job. Luckily, you are soon promoted to the job of high-scaler. The high-scalers hang from the top of the canyon at the end of ropes. They use jackhammers to drill holes in the rock. The holes are filled with dynamite. After the charges explode, the high-scalers clear away loose rock with a crowbar to leave a clean, solid surface for the dam walls to rest against.

WORKING AS A mucker is a backbreaking job, and it has to be done quickly. Trucks are waiting to carry away the rock and mud.

18

Handy Hint

Don't work as a high-scaler if you're afraid of heights.

Bong!

WORKERS MAKE their own safety helmets by dipping soft hats in hot tar. When the tar cools, it hardens. The men call their homemade safety equipment hard-boiled hats, or hard hats. They prevent a lot of injuries.

19

Pouring Concrete

Pouring the concrete begins on June 6, 1933. The high-scalers have almost finished their work, so you are moved to one of the concrete crews. The concrete is made in two nearby production plants built specifically for the job. Giant buckets, each carrying 16 tons (14.5 metric tons) of concrete, are lowered by cable to teams of "puddlers." When the doors at the bottom of a bucket swing open, the concrete gushes out and the puddlers spread it. Cold water is pumped through pipes embedded in the concrete. This keeps the concrete cool and stops it from cracking while it sets.

AT THE BEGINNING OF 1932, the government orders the workers to move to the new town of Boulder City. Everyone is eager to leave the tents and shacks, so Ragtown is soon deserted.

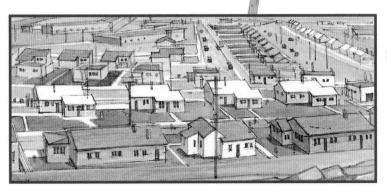

BOULDER CITY has been built by the government and the construction company 7 miles (11 km) from Ragtown to house the dam workers.

Handy Hint

Don't stand still in wet concrete for too long or you'll get stuck!

Gloop!

Whoops! I'd better get moving.

Finishing Up!

THE LAST BUCKET of concrete is poured at the top of the dam on May 29, 1935. The work is finished two years ahead of schedule and under budget.

We did it!

A New Lake

The rock and soil that were dumped to block the river are taken away by trucks and the ends of the diversion tunnels are blocked. The Colorado River now flows toward the dam for the first time. The giant concrete wall stands firm as the water slowly rises behind it. This creates a huge new lake, which is named Lake Mead. By 1939, Lake Mead holds more than 8 trillion gallons (30 trillion liters) of water. By 1941, it is 580 feet (177 m) deep and stretches 120 miles (193 km) upstream behind the dam.

AS LAKE MEAD FILLS UP behind the dam, Ragtown's tents and shacks disappear forever beneath the rising water.

Handy Hint

Don't take a nap beside the rising lake water or you'll get wet!

IF THE WATER ever rises too high behind the dam, spillways let it flow away safely.

LOCAL PEOPLE are soon enjoying the new lake. They use it for sailing, fishing, swimming, and waterskiing.

Powerhouse

Hoover Dam doesn't just supply water and protect against floods—it also makes electricity. Power and water from the Hoover Dam make it possible for new businesses to come to the region and for farmers to irrigate their land and grow more crops. Car, aircraft, textile, and chemical manufacturers move in, providing thousands of jobs and attracting more people to live in the area.

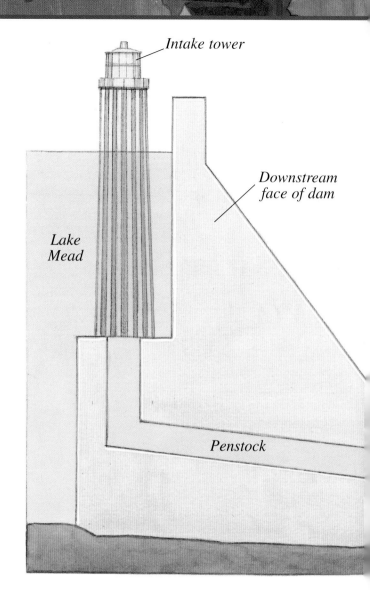

Lake Mead

Intake tower

Downstream face of dam

Penstock

HUGE TOWERS 395 feet (120 m) high channel water from the lake around the dam to the powerhouses on the other side.

WHEN THE LAKE FILLS UP, water pours into the towers and rushes to the powerhouse turbines at a speed of 85 mph (137 kph).

POWERHOUSES on each side of the canyon are fitted with rows of generators to produce electricity.

Handy Hint

Stay away from the power cables. If you touch them, you will light up like a Christmas tree.

Powerhouse

Power cables

Generator

Colorado River

Outflow

Turbine

Making Electricity

WATER from Lake Mead flows around the dam to two rows of turbines, one on each side of the canyon. The rushing water makes the turbines spin. The spinning turbines drive generators, which make electricity.

It's the world's biggest hydroelectric power plant.

HUGE PIPES funnel water from the lake into the powerhouses. They are called penstocks, and are 30 feet (9 m) across.

Opening Day

The completion of the dam is marked by a dedication ceremony on September 30, 1935. Thousands of people gather at the dam to hear a speech by President Franklin Roosevelt. Many of them are workers who helped to build the dam. They bring their families with them for a festive day out in the sunshine. The children finally see what their fathers have been working on. The dam has cost $50 million in 1931 dollars, or about $700 million today. However, higher wages, more expensive machinery, and safer work practices today would probably push the cost up to at least $4 billion.

THE NEW PRESIDENT, Franklin D. Roosevelt, signals to start the first generator at the Hoover Dam on September 11, 1936, by pressing a golden key in Washington, D.C.

Changing Names

BOULDER DAM

WHEN THE PROJECT BEGAN, the dam was called Boulder Dam, because it was meant to be built at Boulder Canyon. (It was actually built at Black Canyon.)

AT A 1930 SPIKE-DRIVING ceremony to begin building the railroad to the construction site, Secretary of the Interior Ray L. Wilbur surprises everyone by naming the dam after then-president Herbert Hoover.

The Hoover Dam!

Handy Hint

Take lots of photographs—you're witnessing a historic moment.

BOULDER DAM

HOO

ON MAY 8, 1933, the new secretary of the interior, Harold Ickes, changes the name back to Boulder Dam.

HOOVER DAM

BOUL

A TWO-LANE HIGHWAY is built along the top of the dam. Eventually, more than 14,000 vehicles will cross it every day.

CONGRESS changes the name back yet again in 1947. It's been the Hoover Dam ever since.

Tourism

You return to the Hoover Dam nearly 30 years later with your grandchildren and go on a guided tour with a group of tourists. Seeing the dam again fills you with pride and brings lots of memories flooding back.

The dam is still a major tourist attraction today, more than 70 years after its construction. Seven million visitors come to see it every year, and another 10 million visit Lake Mead. Boulder City, where the construction workers lived, is still there, too. Today it has a population of about 15,000.

The Hoover Dam Today

1,244 feet (379 m)

726 feet (221 m)

There's enough concrete in the dam to make a road from San Francisco to New York City.*

THE HOOVER DAM is still one of the biggest hydroelectric power plants in the world. With new turbines, it now has a capacity of 2,080 megawatts, enough to supply more than a million homes.

San Francisco

2,500 miles (4,000 km)

New York City

THE HOOVER DAM is called an arch-gravity dam, because it's curved like an arch and its weight holds it in position.

*The road would be 16 feet (4.9 m) wide and more than 2,500 miles (4,000 km) long.

And your great-grandpa helped to build it!

THE ROAD along the top of the dam was closed in 2010 because of safety concerns. A spectacular new road bridge was built to replace it, giving tourists a great view of the dam.

YEARS FROM NOW, your descendants will be able to admire your great achievement.

29

Glossary

Arch-gravity dam A curved dam that stays in position because of its weight.

Canyon A steep-sided river valley.

Congress The lawmaking body of the United States.

Crowbar A strong metal lever.

Dam A barrier built across a river to trap water.

Generator A machine that makes electricity.

High-scaler A construction worker who worked high up on the canyon walls removing loose rock.

Hydroelectric power plant A power station that produces electricity from flowing water.

Investors People who buy shares in a company in the hope that they will rise in value.

Irrigate To water land so that crops can grow on it.

Jackhammer A pneumatic (air-powered) drilling machine used for breaking up rock.

Laborer A person who does heavy physical work that does not require much skill, such as digging or shifting soil.

Latrine A simple toilet consisting of a trench or pit dug in the ground.

Megawatt A unit of electrical power equal to one million watts.

Mucker A worker who scraped rock, soil, and mud off the bottom of the tunnels built to divert the Colorado River.

Penstock A pipe that carries water from a reserve area to a hydroelectric power station. It can also mean a gate that controls the flow of water.

Powerhouse or **power plant** A building in which electricity is produced.

Power shovel A digging machine with a bucket on a mechanical arm.

Puddler A worker who spread out wet concrete.

Ragtown The nickname for the town of tents where dam workers and their families lived at the beginning of the project.

Secretary of commerce The head of the U.S. government's Department of Commerce, which oversees business and industry in the United States.

Secretary of the interior The head of the U.S. government's Department of the Interior, which monitors the supply of energy and the protection of America's natural resources.

Spike-driving ceremony A special event when a long nail or "spike" is hammered into a wooden railroad tie to mark the beginning or end of work on a railroad track.

Spillway A channel that lets water run away from a dam to prevent it from overflowing.

Stock exchange A place where shares in companies are bought and sold.

Surveyor A person who makes very accurate measurements of the position, height, and shape of land.

Turbine A machine that uses flowing water (or steam) to make a shaft spin. The spinning shaft can drive another machine, such as a generator.

Under budget Costing less than expected.

U.S. Reclamation Service A government agency that oversees water supply, dams, water reserves, and hydroelectric power in the United States. Today it is known as the Bureau of Reclamation.

Wall Street The center of New York's financial district.

Index